HALFWAY TO
HELL AND BACK

HALFWAY TO HELL AND BACK

A kick-start for Recovery of
Alcohol and Drug Addiction

Gary N. Laursen

To order additional copies of this book, contact:
Xlibris Corporation
1-888-795-4274
www.Xlibris.com
Orders@Xlibris.com
96495

CONTENTS

INTRODUCTION

Have you ever known an alcoholic or a drug addicted person? Have you ever been one? Well I am here to tell you it is really no fun even though it seems to be at the time. Life is awesome being sober! Here is my story of going *HALFWAY TO HELL AND BACK*. A story about gaining awareness and admitting there may be a problem in your life and how to get back to normal *if* you are ready.

You can read books, talk to friends and family, go to counselors, shrinks, watch films, do intervention, go into a treatment program, and go to AA and NA, read books that offer a cure, or bang your head against the freaking wall and really nothing helps until **YOU** are ready to stop the junk. Of course you will never be ready until you **ADMIT** you have a problem. For me I am a confirmed alcoholic who has drank and used drugs for 25 years and now it has been 25 years since I have NOT had a drink or used drugs.

I did not belong to a gang or go out and hurt people or commit terrible crimes or shoot up. I am not a doctor or a psychiatrist or a counselor. I am just a regular person like you who wants to help if I can. If you have gotten this far by now in my story then I may have got your attention. Maybe this is the greatest day in your life. You really have to be an alcoholic or addict to understand what I am talking about here even though you may not admit it at this moment. Go ahead and read on through—it will be your test—see if you have any similar experiences and then you can answer to yourself when you are ready.

If today or someday you realize there is a problem and say to yourself *"This crap is messing up my life"* then you are on the road to success of making this world a great place to be and to feel good being there. What you are doing is *admitting* you have a problem—that simple. Now the next part is to actually quit which is easy because you have already taken the biggest step of all by admitting there is a problem. When you admit to the problem of alcohol or drug abuse and addiction *then* it is OK to talk to the shrink, the counselor, the friend, intervention, family members, your priest, go to a treatment program, AA or NA meetings, talk to God, Buddha, an idol, just stop on your own, or what ever works for you and then you are ready! That is *if* you are ready. Maybe it is still too fun or you can not live without it, you are sick without it, or it makes your social life useless without it, or your sex life does not exist without it, or your life is not complete without using, then you do have a problem and maybe you are not ready.

Even though we have not met I have tender feelings for you and I am not angry with you and I want to help you. But I can **NOT** help you because it is **YOUR** decision, not mine or anybody else's. Oh yeah I have been there and back so I really have had the experience and know what to do. But now the choice is yours and nobody else's. And like you I too have heard before it is always one day at a time—well I take that back—wrong—one second at a time is more like it. You are always going to have the addiction but it is up to you to control it. I was told once the meaning of an alcoholic or person with any addiction: *"Any time alcohol or any other substance causes a problem in your life then you are an alcoholic or addict"*. This is something to think about, and then think about again, and again.

I did not become an alcoholic because my Grandfather was one or my mother and father were one or my uncle was one or my sister or my friends. I did not inherit it from them nor did they force me into it. It is not a disease I caught from them or my friends. It was something I did on my own—it was my decision and nobody else's. Yes I was dependant on the drugs and alcohol and yes I was addicted. I know this because one day I looked at my life and could see I was having problems. Some say alcohol is a disease—well I am not a doctor but I had never heard of a disease that made you change your personality, laugh, be stupid and drunk or make you want to kill yourself. There just could be a difference between addiction and disease.

As you read my story you will see what I have gone through and you can think of the things you have gone through. You know what they are so make your own list. Your list will be different from mine. And if you have the strength be aware and admit you have a problem. Then you can quit the booze and drugs then you will never want to do this crap again, not even once or you will be right back where you started from. Remember—the *worse* day in your life being sober will be better than your *best* day in your life when you were drinking and/or using drugs.

Please read my story and see if you admit you have a problem. If you do not admit you have a problem then maybe you don't and just go ahead and slip on down to your favorite club or bar and meet with your friends and have a drink or do some drugs—but only ONE and then go on home and don't do it again for another year. Then you probably do not have a problem and really do not need to read my story unless you are not just quite sure—just curious . . . or want to share it with someone you know who just might have a problem . . .

CHAPTER ONE

Early Childhood Days

It all started when I was born back in 1943—or maybe before I was born . . .

My father was born in 1912 and shortly thereafter his family moved to Bend, Oregon. My Grandmother was pregnant with my father as they left their homeland in Denmark to come to the USA. I am told they were especially thrilled as a poor family to have gained passage on the maiden voyage of the *Titanic*. Shortly after boarding the *Titanic* a "Government" person approached them and said there were too many people on board and they would have to leave. They were given passage for another ship and had a safe voyage to the USA and were heartbroken to have not been able to travel on the maiden voyage of the Titanic. Of course they found out later how lucky they were as they heard the news of the Titanic sinking to the ocean floor. Four months later after the trip my father was born. I sometimes think this is where it all started out for me.

During the Second World War my parents left Bend where my father went to Long Beach California to do his part of the war effort by working in the shipyards as a carpenter. During the war in the Los Angeles area if anyone were to drive at night they were not allowed to use lights for fear of enemy aircraft to see the lights and attack the city. My father was a heavy drinker. So the night I decided to be born and to see the light of day my father drove my mother to the hospital without lights on the old Model A Ford. I was told it was a foggy summer evening there in San Pedro. With no lights and the fog my father took a wrong turn and went through the local park and drove that Model A Ford right into the ocean. He got the car back on to the land and off to the hospital just in the nick of time. Since that time my fondest memories of the ocean have been from the shore.

My parents were good parents and taught me well but we were a dysfunctional family always struggling to survive. I was one of those little boys with a baby face, slender, quiet and reserved, you may say shy. I was not invited to the birthday parties and Valentines

Day was a nightmare for me. The other kids called me a wimp and picked on me and bullied me a lot. The first day of the first grade some kid slugged me in the stomach and I went home crying and did not want to go back. My school years never were happy times and I took little interest.

My father built homes for a living and got started from saving war bonds during WWII. We barely survived with his business as homes were hard to sell. Starting at age five I helped him as a clean up person for 5 Cents and hour. As time went on I graduated to learning carpentry.

I also had a few experiences with religion. When I was in the 3rd grade I had a friend who had asked me to go to church with him at a little church across from Kenwood School on Newport Avenue in Bend, Oregon. The next time I went to church was another Church in Bend on 3rd street, which was not paved at that time but an oiled dirt road. It later became a well known Italian Restaurant. I went there and became involved with church the activities. I remember how I would walk there every Sunday from our home about a mile away. I also remember walking home late in the evening in the dark after the evening youth activities and how scared I was going through where Oaks Square is with the old houses which seemed to be making noises at me when I then "Ran like crazy" past them to get home.

I would save up my money and remember one time I put 50 cents in the offering. I remember the good feeling I got from giving as I felt I was really doing something good. But then my friend who wanted me to go to church with him would take the wooden bowl as it came by and he would tap the bottom of the bowl and at the same time reach in and take out some money while pretending to put money in the bowl. This kind of ended my religious times. I was not always a good kid and ran with the kids who got into trouble. I seemed to choose the wrong friends and got into trouble with but never anything really serious.

Shortly thereafter our family moved to Redmond and being a fourth grader and being grown up (at least I thought) any spare moments were taken with helping my father build homes. Times were tough at that time and we lived in very humble conditions. We were a poor dysfunctional family to say the least. Besides helping my father I would go to the railroad tracks and pick up potatoes off the ground where they had fallen off of the overloaded railroad cars. This was our food. There were times when I would go through the alleys on Saturday and Sunday morning and go through the garbage cans and search for bottles from homes where

I knew there were parties the night before. Yes I would roam around on Friday and Saturday nights and listen for people making a lot of noise by yelling or fighting or loud music with a lot of people coming and going at certain homes.

The next morning I would check out the garbage cans in the alleys or knock on their door and ask for the empties. These people mostly in their early twenties sure seemed happy when they were partying but the next morning they looked really sick. The grange hall by the local airport was also a good take the morning after the Saturday night dance because you could not drink inside so everyone went to their cars to drink and threw the empties out in the sagebrush. You would get 1 cent for a beer bottle and 3 cents for a pop bottle. These were my targets the next day for my booty. Sometimes I would make over $5.00 in a day and at that time the minimum wage was less than a dollar an hour for an adult. I also learned the hard work of harvesting potatoes and giving my earnings to my parents for food. I will never forget the cold day I sold my bicycle for $5.00 to get food for my family. I was not resentful to help the family. It actually made me feel good. Part of the $5.00 went for cigarettes and beer for my parents and I was fine with that too.

We continued to live in three room motels. I had a sister who was four years older than I who gave me no support and laughed at any of my goals and called me stupid and stole from me and made me feel like an idiot. My other sister being two years older than I was also abused by the older sister and she gave me it seems the only support I could ever remember at least till she became a grown up teenager. I did poorly in school with bad grades. I hated school—it sucked. I did not feel good about myself. I remember my mother telling me when I was 10 years old that I had an inferiority complex. When I asked her what that meant she said I felt everyone was better than me—that I felt everyone was superior to me. She was right and the comment just amplified those feelings.

During the 8th grade the Mormon Missionaries came by and told us about the book of Mormon and we talked about the scriptures and beliefs and things. I was really interested but the missionaries never came back again because dad would not give up his beer each night and Mom would not give up her Pall Mall cigarettes nor would they give up their coffee. I decided I wanted to go to a church again so I went to the Mormon Church two Sundays in a row. I went with my 17 year old sister who was four years older than me and her husband. I asked my brother in law at the time why he wanted to go to church. He said the chorister was really hot and he wanted to check her out. Of course he was also trying to pick up on the Junior High girls at the same time. A few years later he got mixed up with a drug crowd and got shot and killed. We were living in Prineville then. I went to their church meeting and after the meeting was the Sunday school. I did not know where to go during the Sunday school time so I thought someone would tell me. I was shy and did not ask anyone. I remember both times it was the same because after the meeting all the people went off to their Sunday School classes so I waited and soon everyone was gone. Just another disappointment and this seemed typical for me. I got up and left and as far as I was concerned I was done with any church for ever. My whole idea about religion was a confusing mess.

CHAPTER TWO

Growing Up

In the 8th grade my mother told me I was a hard worker and that she liked to watch me work as I made every move count. I was thin but strong and could outwork almost any grown man. That was the only thing I felt really good about so I worked very hard to gain praise. At age 13 under my father's supervision and several mistakes I built my first home. It was fun to learn how to build homes and being a part of the construction watching everything from the ground up.

My father built homes on speculation and built sometimes as many as four homes a year. When my father was gone I supervised the workers—they didn't like a 13 year old telling them how to do things so they got angry at me. I continued to work hard and ignored school and dropped out barely completing the

11th grade. I lied about my age and worked for the Forest Service on the fires in the summer and after that it was hard to find work and my father was not building any homes at the time.

Being 16 years old and looking like I was 12 years old must have been a pretty funny sight out there looking for work. So I built furniture and sold it at the auction barn and worked bucking hay on the farms and the potato processing plants. I subcontracted siding installation for a while and it was hard getting paid and hard getting jobs there in the late 50's.

My goal was to be liked but did not know how to go about it. I had only a few friends. Went along with the current fads with the curly hair down into my eyes and wore a shirt with the collar pulled up and my jeans pulled down as far as they would go just trying to be cool. The white socks and black shoes were in style with your jeans tightly rolled up so you could see the socks. You were really cool if you had a pack of Lucky Strikes rolled up in your shirt sleeve. I would try that once in a while even though I did not smoke—yet. If you were wealthy enough you would wear penny loafers with a dime in the slot. The coolest thing was to go out drinking with the guys. I tried to look the part but still did not have the personality for really good friends.

To get a car and drive was my dream, my freedom, my fame, my wealth, my popularity, my chance in life to be recognized and more friends. Just when I turned sixteen my father owed me $300 for working the last eight years at a nickel an hour. It was 1959 and my father had a 1951 Plymouth which he gave me for the owed money. A Plymouth was not the custom street rod type but I fixed it up myself with straight pipes, lakers, lowered and raked, louver hood, all the emblems and chrome gone and filled, a $35 metal flake red paint job and a genuine plastic naugahide interior and had me a genuine home made sort of custom hot rod car. The original old flat head six cylinder never had much power but I had a special way of hitting the brakes when shifting into second gear and the tires would screech and everyone thought it was pretty hot because they thought I was gettin second gear rubber.

I gained a few instant friends and even got a girl friend so put all the success to my beloved car. It was washed and waxed every day and sometimes twice a day. Later I felt the only reason I had the friends was because they got a free ride in my cool car. I got to where I felt I was just being used and maybe I was.

CHAPTER THREE

First Introduction to Alcohol

Then tragedy struck. I had never taken a drink in my entire life so had no clue of the effects of alcohol. It was time for me to be really cool and run around with some of the guys who drank. My good friend Buddy who was from Oklahoma said lets go out and get some booze one Friday evening. The first question was at sixteen years old where do we get it and we had little money anyhow. He had a plan. There was a liquor store and two grocery stores in town. So you just wait across the street from the liquor store and check out the kind of car the person has who had gone into the liquor store for booze. Then you drive over to one of the two grocery stores in town and wait. You had a 50-50 chance the guy would go to one of the grocery stores and pick up some mixer or something on the way home. Sure enough the car we spotted at the liquor store pulled into the Market where we were waiting. Buddy slipped over to the car after the guy went inside and reached under the seat and grabbed the two bottles of booze and we were off to party. In a small Oregon town of about 3,500 populations there were no gangs or major crime. Not like the big city crime but really no different. If you get in trouble it is still trouble or doing something bad is still bad no matter if you are in a big city or a little town.

We got some orange juice to mix with the Vodka. We drank all that booze and just drove around. I really did not realize it was doing anything to me but I really felt strange. Later in the evening I got really dizzy and laid down under a juniper tree and vomited. Buddy came over to help me and I threw him down the hill. Guess it was time to go home. I remember running up to the house and forgot to twist the door knob before hitting the door with my body and ended up bouncing off of it and landing face down on the sidewalk. Went in and vomited the rest of the night. My parents asked me the next morning what happened and I told them I had drunk too much orange juice. They knew better but said nothing. Oh man I was sick. I swore I would never drink again but would never say I had got "drunk" because that was a dirty word.

A few months later it seems I must have changed my mind because I ended up with Buddy again and we did the same thing. He was driving my car and I was in the back seat unable to navigate from too much booze. We went to the local gravel pit with some other guys who had cars and they stole some gas from the excavation equipment while I was sick in the back seat. They had cut off a gas hose to siphon the gas from some equipment and put it into the trunk of my car. A week later Buddy thought the free gas was a great idea so got some of the other guys together with their cars, loaded up some gas cans and the siphon hose in my trunk and here we go off to the gravel pit. As we pulled up to the gas tanks the lights went on and there was this giant of a man standing there with a shotgun pointed two inches from my nose. They hauled us off to jail and I had the opportunity to lose my drivers license for three months as punishment from the judge. I had no idea the alcohol was causing me any trouble just thought it was bad luck.

Doing drugs in the early 60's in small towns was pretty much unknown and totally unacceptable. Of course we never ever thought of alcohol as a drug. Booze was acceptable and drugs were for hippies and weirdoes. Prineville Oregon was a logger and cowboy town actually known as the Cowboy Capital of the World at that time. It was more drink and chew tobacco than real cowboy things but there were some pretty tough cowboys.

CHAPTER FOUR

Off to the Army

I dropped out of High School in the 11th grade being seventeen years old and still looked like I was fourteen. I really never seemed to fit with the other kids in school. I applied for a job as a carpenter at several job sites and they laughed at me when I told them I was a finish carpenter and they told me to get off of their job sites as though I was an annoying little brat. My father was not building homes at that time because the market was not good. I got a job at the carnival and worked for a week and they left and never paid me so gave up on that. Working the farms tossing around bales of hay (bucking bales) was hard for me because I just did not have the strength for this kind of work. I sold the old 51 Plymouth and bought a 55 Chevy which was the dream of my life. I really needed that $39 a month to keep up on the car payments. It was 1961 and I thought if I can not get a good job then maybe it was time for me to do my duty and sign up for the draft. Sure why not I was 17 years old and couldn't get a job anyhow.

Of course I was pushed along by the court. I really wanted some 1956 Buick tail lights for my 55 Chevy—they really looked cool on the 55 Chevy. I was gone one weekend and my buddies decided to get me some Buick Taillights so they gave me this wonderful gift. I popped them on my car and went crusin through Prineville and in less than a minute the cops had me pulled over and arrested me for possession of stolen property. The judge said if I went into the army then he would drop the case. I went to the draft board and had my name put on the top of the draft list. My parents signed for approval which was necessary because I was under eighteen. Just to get the military over with I chose the draft as it was two years instead of the enlisted time being a minimum of three years. A month before my 18th birthday I was drafted into the US Army for a two year period.

A few weeks before I left to the Army I went out with my buddy Dick and we got some beer and drank till I got sick. A pretty uneventful evening but woke up in his front yard vomiting. I remember his parents standing there next to their Studebaker looking at me like I was some kind of an idiot. Guess I was. I was just not good at drinking because I always got sick. But that never stopped me.

I learned a lot of things in the Army. I had never really been away from home. There was a new and interesting vocabulary with a lot of F words which were easy to learn and they were used by everyone (especially the leaders) several times in each sentence. What was really cool was that I could go to the PX which was like an Army store where you could drink beer. No age limit I guess as I was seventeen and if you were in the Army you had to be old enough to drink so to drink and be legal was way cool. There were hundreds of guys standing out on the street drinking beer just standing around. I soon found that drinking made me feel like a real adult; yes a real man and not a baby faced kid. I could lose my shyness, talk louder, use all the swear words, be an asshole, be a jerk, act tough and I thought even romantic at times. I was never a tough guy or a fighter but I did learn to run around with some of the tough guys so others would know they were my buddies and leave me alone.

In basic training I learned to take advantage of any breaks during the heavy workload day during basic training. So on one occasion the officer in charge said

"Smoke Break". So everyone would kick back for ten or fifteen minutes and rest and have a cigarette. I noticed that not everyone was smoking and I was one of those guys. Those who were not smoking were sent to clean the outside toilets. You better believe the next time there was a smoke break I had a pack of cigarettes. The next time there was a break I pulled out my cigarette and put it in my mouth. Thought I had them fooled but the officer in charge said "Private Laursen if you are going to take a smoke break then you had better light it up" go clean toilets . . .The next time I followed all the rules and lit it up and coughed and gagged on those crazy things for the next 25 years. Guess I got more experienced on how to drink alcohol too and became addicted to that poison for the next 25 years as well which nearly took my life many times. I took advantage of the times when we were allowed to go to the PX and drink beer but we only had less than an hour to be there so never got really smashed or sick so figured I had the drinking handled like a pro.

After basic training it was off to Fort Riley Kansas for nine months as a mail clerk. The Army guys drank nearly every night at the PX and I ended up drinking beer till late and then vomiting when we got back to the barracks. This happened nearly every night. The Company commanding officer called me in one morning and had a "chat" with me about the drinking because someone complained. I didn't listen and kept on pounding down those beers. I just figured the vomiting and getting sick were just a part of drinking so I learned to accept being sick.

CHAPTER FIVE

Off to Germany

I got married at age 18 to my high school sweetheart, just before I was shipped off to Germany where I was a clerk in a Construction Battalion. Guess my 11th grade high school education learning how to type was a big plus. I really learned how to drink beer there in Germany. This stuff was 13% alcohol unlike the then wimpy 3.2% American beer. I liked the taste of this beer better than the American beer and seemed like I could drink more but still got sick from it. Again we went out every night and spent any spare time drinking—that was the Army life.

One evening we were at the Church Bar (yes it was a bar attached to a church where the people would have a beer before church and several after church) there in Pirmasens Germany and I was plastered. A guy sitting at our table was trying to convert everyone to Communism which was a big no no to be around especially being in the military. The German bar tender did not take it pleasantly. He was a huge man and he took his fist and hit this Communist guy right on the top of his head. Guess it must have broken his neck or something because the guy just dropped dead right there beside me. The bartender and another German drug him out along the side of the road in the bushes and everyone including the bartender drank the night away. Then wondering every day when I might get arrested by having someone find out and I being possibly involved. Nothing was ever said but I did change places to hang out. Was not realizing the people I hung around would someday get me into real trouble.

It seems I got sick almost every time I drank because I just drank too much. I just felt I did not fit in unless I drank and then I had no limits set on the amount. When the army guys got together it was not to sip on a beer it was always a race on who could drink the most in the shortest period of time. Interesting how the drinking in excess just snuck up on me without even noticing it.

The morning I left Germany to come home from completing my Army time the Battalion Colonel (I was his secretary) came to me and said they were leaving for Vietnam to build bridges and he would like for me to go and they were leaving that morning. The pay would have been over $300 a month and I was tempted because that was a lot more than the $185 I was getting at the time. I had a choice which road to take and decided to come back home even though I was still only nineteen years old and had a wife and needed to be responsible but now looked like sixteen. Later I found out the Colonel did not tell me the whole story in that people would be shooting at us while we were building bridges and many of the men in my battalion would be killed or many of them would get hooked on heroin—maybe he did not know either.

At that time military men were looked down upon like the scum of the earth. While traveling through Chicago with my required uniform on I was standing at the bus depot next to an elderly lady and she said "how dare you stand next to me—"filthy soldier!" I got to dislike the Army and how the soldiers were degraded. I felt I had made the right choice to get discharged from the military and thankfully somehow by means of "an honorable discharge". The drinking could have become an issue in not getting the honorable discharge.

CHAPTER SIX

Civilian Life

Civilian life for a nineteen year old boy having already served his country was different and I was in a hurry to make good in my life. Living in Bend, Oregon the prestigious thing to do was to obviously work in the woods as a logger. I got a job with a local timber company as a knot bumper (where you remove the limbs from the fallen trees with a chain saw) I was pretty excited with my new "White" brand boots and Levi Jacket, suspenders and red sweatshirt all ready to go off to the woods with the loggers. These loggers were really cool and it was known that at the end of the day after working in the woods they would crack open the beers coming back to town in the crummy (a four wheel drive van they rode in). They had me take a physical the evening before I started work. I was unable to pass the vision test as I had a problem with my eyes so they said I could not have the job as it would be dangerous. I was heartbroken to not get this job which paid $2.50 an hour along with all the status which went with it. I mean those loggers stuck together and drank beer every night. A few days later it was on the news about a young man who just started to work for Brooks Willamette as a knot bumper was killed from a logging accident on his first day of the job. Guess it was not my time to go because that was my job.

I had never forgotten the skills my father had taught me for many years of how to be a carpenter so I thought why not try to get a job as a carpenter. After all I was two years older now and finished the service so maybe someone would consider me. A friend told me about John Robbins who was building homes on Bear Creek Road. I went and talked with John and he put me to work as a finish carpenter. I was shocked as he offered me $3.50 per hour. Don't know if I was lucky or just a little BS and a little help from a friend but I did get the job. I had few tools and looked like a kid. Another carpenter who worked for him said if I was going to be a carpenter then I needed to look like one. The first day on the job I had my nice new white carpenter overalls. Smeared them with dirt and beat them on the rocks for a while to make me look like I had a lot of experience. I was with the home builder for the next two years. I learned a lot there from some of the other guys who had more experience than me.

Not only did I learn the trade better but I learned more about my drinking career with my working buddies every evening and weekends. I was then 20 and the drinking age was 21 but my working buddies managed to get me into the tavern anyhow. I never admitted of being an alcoholic because I never drank the hard stuff. Because if you drank the hard stuff you were considered to have a drinking problem nor did I ever admit to being "drunk" but being a little tipsy I would always say.

Then it was off to start my own business building homes. I sold my fix it upper home in Bend and walked out of the title company with $3,500 nearly doubling my money and moved to Prineville. My young wife and I had two children, a girl and a boy. Those children were awesome! My daughter I called Blondie and she was an angel. My son Neil was a carbon copy of me—I was dad and friend all in one. I worked hard there in that little city and did a lot of building for the next 10 years and did a lot of drinking it up.

CHAPTER SEVEN

Graduating to Hard Liquor

I was not always one of those get drunk 24 hours a day type guys as I would go out just about every night and close the bars at 1:00 in the morning and then go home, vomit, get some sleep and then get up at 6:30 then vomit some more and go to work. The weekends were different—I eventually learned to drink 24 hours a day. Later on I was able to master the art of what I called "being a professional drinker" and do the drinking every waking moment with sometimes what we called a three day drunk. Never admitted there was a problem as there was always an excuse for me to drink. You know like it was raining or it was not raining or snowing or too cold or too hot.

If it was bad weather we would all go on down to the tavern at 7:30 in the morning and start pounding down beers and non stop till closing time. The term for that was to vote it dry. Now don't get me wrong I was also a respected citizen in the community with my building homes and helping out charitable organizations. Of course with those charitable organizations everyone drank before during and after any event. I even took first place in the World Championship Jeep Rodeo in 1969. I could still function then.

It seemed the only way I could have friends was to drink. I really felt I had to drink. I didn't know someone could have any fun without drinking. I thought it was necessary to go to the taverns or the Pioneer Club or the Elks Club and drink with the guys. Just felt it was a part of my home building business and being necessary. Even convinced my wife it was necessary and she went along often.

My grandfather taught me how to make home brew which tasted kind of like the German beer and just as powerful. I made 105 bottles of this stuff every week for five years and drank it all along with the help of a few friends and of course still hitting the bars at the same time. The beer got to where it just made me full and took a lot to get a buzz. I finally graduated to the hard stuff and it would not be uncommon to hop in the pickup at 9:00 in the morning with my brother in law Buckshot and one of his cowboy or logger buddies with a couple of fifths of Black Velvet and a half case of beer. The first thing was to take the cap off that whiskey bottle and toss it out the window. It was a tradition to toss the cap. Why bother with the cap because the bottle would be empty in a short time anyhow so why bother with screwing that cap on and off. All my friends drank and they loved to take advantage of me in any way they could. Yup I would buy those guys drinks while the other friends were at the job sites stealing materials from my job.

I could write a full length novel about the experiences drinking there in Prineville. It seemed funny at the time but now I look back and it seems sad. It seems all my friends were heavy drinkers and I ran around with the rowdy cowboys and loggers and even got beat up a time or two. Running with those guys I felt safe because other people were afraid of them. My best cowboy buddy had shot and killed a guy in a gunfight in the parking lot behind the Pastime but never got any jail time because it was determined to have been a fair fight. I found my friends were not the nicest people in the world. I later found out *you are who your friends are.*

I really do not know how I was able to get jobs doing building projects other than I was priced low and had some good design ideas. Most of the rest of the town were big drinkers too so it was kind of acceptable there. At that time everything involved with the drinking seemed funny and like a joke.

CHAPTER EIGHT

Trouble with the Law

I was able to avoid drunken driving tickets somehow. But did get stopped by the cops many times and somehow talked my way out of a ticket. I even managed to get my name in the local newspaper now and then. Where me and this other guy was out in the mountains in my Jeep and (drinking) came across an old miners cabin and my friend shot a hole in the middle of his wood stove with a shotgun (I never liked him for that) and we got picked up and thrown in jail. We got out of that one because the cops forgot to read our legal rights. Or the one where my brother in law Buckshot and I got thrown in jail when he stole a velvet painting of a nude Mexican girl from the Rustlers Roost Bar one day when we were on one of those three day drunks. Hmm—interesting how I still do not like the word "drunk" and at that time still never admitted to being drunk. Or the time I outran the State, City and County police in my pickup on the back roads where they had recognized me and got me the next day.

Or the one where I had been drinking for two days and got tired and sick and asked one of my drinking buddies down at the Horse Shoe Tavern to drive me home as I could not function enough to drive. Then he says how am I going to get back? So I said just take my pickup (which was only two years old). Not a good choice because he left then picked up his buddies and they went for a joy ride and totaled it out on McKay Creek Road and the wreck sent them all to the hospital. Nobody died but it was a wonder. I found out about it on the local radio news the next morning. I went to look at the wrecked pickup at the wrecking yard and the dash was smashed all to pieces and here were all these beer and whiskey caps which had gone down into the windshield defroster then scattered all over the cab. There were hundreds of them.

Or the one where I was to judge the parade exhibits while being a member of the Jaycees and gave first prize to a group of babes riding on a hay wagon from the hair stylist place. The local department store was pissed as they got second place. They had

Clydesdale horses shipped in and spent a fortune each year on the parade exhibit. They had won first place for ever and they never entered again because the babes got first prize and spent nothing. Or the one where me and another guy were driving the ambulance as a volunteer during the local Rodeo—a rider fell off his horse so the announcer and the fans were yelling "where is the ambulance". I and the other guy driving the ambulance were out back getting a refill on our beer—where else. Or the time when a friend and I were out at the Lakeview Saloon and left at closing. I took a left and drove home and my friend went straight and within a block he ran into the back of a parked logging truck and it cut his head off.

There were times when I was smart enough to let a friend drive. There was once after leaving the Pioneer Club my buddy was driving my pickup and got stopped. While he was doing the drunken driving test I asked one of the cops if I could borrow his cop car and go do some cookies out in the sagebrush. Guess he thought I was kidding because he said go ahead—so I really had a ball out there with that cop car—lights flashing, siren going with the sagebrush and dirt flying all over this vacant lot. They sent us on our way because they probably didn't want anyone to find out as they may have lost their jobs.

There was another time with a friend driving where we got stopped by the cop's downtown. The cops asked me to get out of the pickup and I said something smart to them and they pulled me out of the car, took me to the ground and smacked my shins with a bully club. Man that hurt like crazy and I still have dents in my legs to prove it. Anyhow they hauled us off to jail. They put me in a jail cell by myself apparently to sober me up. Prineville has always been famous for nobody having ever escaped from their jail and it still is. Well it just so happened they did not take my pocket knife from me and I was able to remove the lock from the door. Walked through the jail with nobody around to see me and came up to the counter where the dispatcher was. I knew her because she was my drinking buddy's mother. Said how's it going and then I said not too bad—guess I better be on my way and she said goodbye Gary have a nice day. You have a nice day too ma'am and off I go.

I got a visit from the chief of police around noon the next day. He says Gary you know it is election time and he would say nothing about the breakout if I said nothing and if I would fix the lock. I said OK and fixed the lock and went on my way feeling pretty cocky about getting by with my drinking escapades with no real trouble or jail time.

There was a law introduced called the open container law. This was where you were in violation of the law if you had an open bottle of alcohol in your vehicle. So the trick was to toss the empties in the back of the pickup. It was crazy when you would stop or take off and all those bottles and cans would roll around and make all kinds of racket and break. Even got a few tickets for not getting all the whiskey drank in time before tossing the empty in the back. Yeah if you saw a cop it was important to drink all the booze as fast as you could and finish it and toss it in the back so you would not get busted for the open container law and at the same time to not waste any of that precious stuff. Have no idea why I never got busted for a DUI—at least up to that point.

A birthday represents the number of years you have spent on earth. When you are young—it was for me anyhow saying from age one to 21 each birthday signified one year closer to being an adult, freedom or some kind of status or personal goals being reached. Being 21 was my earlier goal and I think it was because I would no longer be treated like a kid. Of course everyone has their own definition of being an adult. I am not sure what my definition is. Mine was being of age to drink. Yes, I am serious. Then when you reach 21 each birthday means you made it one more year.

Then I would think there was the negative side saying you are one more year closer to the proverbial death. As for me I felt I would not live much past 30 for what ever reason. I mean like I felt I would never make it to 31. So I felt each day I was living on borrowed time and needed to make the best of it. Like let's get crazy and do all the stupid things most people never get the chance to do as well as many of the things we never did and wanted to do. The alcohol gave me the desire and courage to do all these crazy things. Like stealing the beer truck and getting it back before the cops came. Money was not an issue because there always seemed to be money even when you were broke to support the habits.

There was always a reason to drink. Something good happened, something bad happened, someone died, someone was born, a holiday, Tuesday afternoon, it didn't matter because there was always an excuse or a reason why I needed to take that drink and once I took a drink there was no stopping. Oh no it was never my fault or my decision it was just something I was supposed to do—at least which was what I thought in my warped mind. Of course the moment I had one drink it did not stop till the bars closed and usually long past that. The drinking progressed and eventually ruined my marriage.

I lost my wife and my two children but I never lost my craving for alcohol and the "hard stuff" became no problem and even found myself experimenting with drugs a little. I had no responsibilities because my wife and family were gone. Figured it was a good time to buy a used Corvette and waste what ever savings I had left. On Thanksgiving Day went down to the local Pastime Club in the middle of town pounding down some Black Velvet shots. I was with one of my tough cowboy buddies and we looked at the Corvette parked in front and I said—I have always wanted to go through town at 100 miles per hour and run the stop light (there was only one stop light in Prineville then). So we hopped in the Corvette and did just that—was a wonder we did not get killed or at least spend Thanksgiving in jail but the cops must have had the day off and nobody driving through town to get run over by a whacked out Corvette. We went back to the Pastime and continued to put em down. Yeeeee Hawwwww!

CHAPTER NINE

Off to the Big City

The time building in Prineville lasted about ten years till the booze finally took over my building business and I lost everything.

It was time to move away and have the life I never had, to be single and experience life as I thought I should have before I got married at 18. I look at it now and see how selfish I was. I sold everything and had a pocket full of money. What the heck I was 33 years old. Off to the big city and **Party Time**!

Boise Idaho was waiting with some new friends down at the local "Outlaw Club" in Garden City which I found the minute I got into town. Found some great friends there who were truck drivers and wannabe cowboys. They did not mind to start the drinking in the afternoon and continue till the morning and beyond.

One of the guy's girlfriends (her name was Reno Donna) says to me quote "Gary you are no fun unless you have been drinking". I really took her seriously because the next nine years I made it a point to be *"more fun"*. There was not a day that passed where I was not drunk but of course still never ever admitted to the term of being drunk. I built a couple homes the first couple of years and then seemed to not be able to get any work at all doing building or anything else for that matter. My money ran out and I totaled out the Corvette.

Once I started getting the drunken driving tickets I continued to get them. I got busted often and in one week I got busted once for drugs, once for a DUI and once for a car wreck. Did a little jail time with some negotiating and promises which I did not keep and wonder why I never got any hard time. Had it been today it would have been different because the law is not so generous today.

For a short time I had a girlfriend who asked me to go to an AA meeting. I went with her to that meeting just to keep her happy and not that I wanted to go because *I* did not have an alcohol problem. At the meeting there was a guy there who talked about how he got drunk and climbed a tree and fell asleep in the tree. He spoke of how he woke up in this tree and was afraid and screamed for someone to help him down. He said something about this being his awareness of him having a problem. I thought it was pretty funny and just laughed at his story and went on not knowing or understanding what he was really trying to say. That this was his time to recognize he had a problem—he was admitting. It took many years for me to get to that point but his tree climbing experience I never forgot and one day "I climbed my tree" as well.

My then13 year old son came to live with me because my ex wife felt she was not doing a good job with him. Well she was doing a much better job than I could have done and by me being a poor example I continually blame myself up to this day for ruining his life. It seems the alcohol became more important than anything. I invested all my money with my older sister in a venture she and her husband were promoting and the rest I invested in booze. The investment with my sister was a scam that got me and several others and I should have known better from my years growing up with her when she stole from me when I was a little kid. I felt then I had good reasons to drink even more.

After a few years in Boise I heard of someone who wanted a house built. Because I had drunken driving tickets with no drivers license was unable to drive so rode my bicycle to the client's home—Went there the morning after a night of drinking and it seems all I did was stand there and stutter—they asked me to leave—what a sight I must have been. It was then that I decided I was no longer a home builder—heck with it and off to the liquor store.

CHAPTER TEN

Introduction to Drugs

Like I said before the drugs in the small cowboy town were not acceptable but they sure were in the big city. Some of the truck driver buddies did drugs and I also got to running around with some biker guys. Started smoking a little pot and it made me laugh but it was hard for me to navigate. After a couple of years of smoking pot I could not think straight and got into this terrible paranoid feeling. If I was driving I would stop the car and hide in the back or if home would go under the house and hide. It was so weird but still smoked when the buddies passed it around.

Then along came this new song "Driving that train, high on cocaine, Casey Jones is ready, watch your speed" by the Grateful Dead. I tried this cocaine and it did not take long to figure out this stuff was awesome!

I mean I felt good and I could drink and do coke for days. It even seemed to keep me from getting sick from the booze. It was amazing how the coke made me smarter, sexier and I could talk and talk and really think I made a lot of sense and really feel smart with not a care in the world! I could drink all I wanted and still function and no big deal to smoke four packs of cigarettes a day.

The only problem with the cocaine is there was not enough of it and it was expensive. It was typical to share with friends so a gram only lasted minutes and it was gone and then off to find some more. Of course it was cheaper to buy and eight ball (1/8 ounce) so always tried to buy it in that size or the ¼ ounce. When I bought it that way I could re-sell some of it and hopefully get mine for free. I learned that when you sell it you had the right to cut it. I would take out the fresh coke and would buy baby laxative which was preferred and mix it in with the coke and I would keep the fresh stuff for me. Then you would always short the weight by 10% and then blame the scale if anyone complained. When I sold any of the white stuff it was always normal for the buyer to give a line or two to the seller so this dealing stuff was getting pretty cool. That did not last long because it came to pass that I cut it more and more and people did not like it and did not pay. The whole idea in selling and being a low level dealer was to make a few bucks by selling the cut coke but then I only used it instead of selling it. Following that became the problems with my dealer.

I owed my dealer a bunch of money for coke. To pay off some of the debt we made a deal for me to come over to his house and remodel his basement for some of the payment. I was building a bar in the basement and had to run some framing down from the ceiling for the bar. There was an opening in the ceiling with a makeshift cover on it and I pulled the cover off and down dropped about a pound of cocaine in a zip-lock bag. It was like it came from heaven. That stuff was pure as could be and I helped myself till he walked in. He grabbed it up and walked away. He was a big guy and could have killed me but he needed a lot of more work done on his house.

The dealing coke was not doing well. Almost got busted once with trying to sell an ounce but my dealer heard on the police scanner they had a sting operation out and it fit me to a tee. I did not continue with the deal which was good because I would probably still be in the slammer for that one. I would have gotten caught for sure.

I met up with a guy I knew who worked at the grocery store and he said he wanted $25 worth of coke and asked if I had some. I said sure but I really had none but still really needed some money. I went out to my car and crunched up some aspirin and put it into one of those cute little paper envelope containers and sold it to him.

One of my coke dealers also worked at the local lumber yard and hardware store as a salesman. The hint to buying was for the customer to request white paint in a pint or a quart or a gallon. The pint was a gram and the quart was an eight ball and the gallon was a quarter ounce. This town must have had a lot of users because he sold more dollars of cocaine out the doors of that huge lumber yard every day than all of the lumber and hardware put together. He was living the high life and it was fine with me when he wanted to share any of his "spare" coke.

Then came the free-basing (crack) of the coke which I also liked which seemed to go farther but the buzz disappeared really quick. I still loved the coke because I could just drink it seemed forever, sometimes for days and days at a time to never sleep or eat because the coke took my appetite away.

Then a friend introduced me to heroine. I had been drinking and doing coke for nearly three days straight. When we smoked that heroine it was awesome and I felt like I was on top of the world. Actually it felt so good it scared me and for some reason I never did it again. I did not realize how lucky I was at the time. I tried mushrooms, peyote, acid, hash and anything else that would come along but the booze and coke were my favorites.

CHAPTER ELEVEN

Hiding Out

It was cold that winter when my 16 year old son and I were living in that little house in Boise. We hadn't paid the rent or paid the power or gas bill for months. Many windows were broken out; the wind blew a chill through that house. There was a green plant in the living room which always stayed green. It was so cold for months and I couldn't figure out why it was always green. The moment we got kicked out of the house and moved that plant finally got into some warmth it turned black. Then I realized the plant had been frozen inside our house for months. We needed money so I went to a local church begging for some money and they seemed to be interested only in me giving them money which I did not have so I never went back there. We were able to con the State into giving out some food stamps for a few months. The food stamps could only be used to buy food and not any booze or cigarettes. When you get the food stamps you go into the grocery store and buy food with them and then stand outside the grocery store entrance door and have these bags of food for sale—all for half price. It only took a few minutes and the food was sold and off to buy the booze and maybe hook up with a little coke.

I got drunken driving tickets every time I turned around. My luck had run out on not getting busted. One day after drinking a six hour or so lunch with a friend I got stopped by the cops and was not even able to do the street tests like counting or touching your nose. They pegged me for a .035 blood alcohol test which some say you would be legally dead. This got me a real good ticket and the judge sentenced me to a few days of jail and to go to AA meetings every week for a year and professional counseling for a year and then to get a full report at the end of the year for evaluation. I never went to any of it—just said the hell with it as I had better things to do.

My son and I ended up in a cabin up in the mountains someone had loaned us. Still penniless and still able to get drugs and alcohol every day—somehow—I will never know how. We stayed there till the snow got so deep and it was so cold we had to go. With no money for food or a place to live it was to sponge off of anyone who would take pity. Oh yes for an alcoholic and drug addict it is always possible to get some stash. My son was hooked on pot and every other drug imaginable and went back to where his mom was in Portland. I had some bad biker guys after me from some "business" deals which had gone sour. It seems I always kept a step ahead. I headed off to a job in Maine as a laborer on a job installing equipment in a potato processing plant. You guessed it with my old friend Buddy.

Trying to hide from the biker gang my days were no different than before only I had a job. I was unable to function well because of the booze and drugs. At times I showed up to work either drunk or high and there was the coke and booze for lunch time. I never got fired because the rest of the crew including the bosses was doing the same thing. I left Maine after a few months and ended up in Caldwell, Idaho working on another potato processing plant with the same company. Still had the fist full of drunken driving tickets and two months left to complete the court ordered sentence of counseling and AA and other meetings which was part of my sentence for the drunken driving tickets. At this point nothing seemed to make any difference and I really didn't care.

CHAPTER TWELVE

Blackouts

I really forgot how many drunken driving tickets there were but think there were four in a short time, and still driving without a valid drivers license. I acquired and lived in the back of a beat up 73 Orange Ford van for over three years. Today they call this being homeless but that old van was my home. It used a quart of oil with each tank of gas. There were times I had lost the van for several days in a row because I started occasionally having blackouts after only a few drinks. One afternoon I looked for it for a full day and found it in the parking lot of a bar with all the doors open and miraculously the keys still in it and nothing stolen. Of course there was not much to steal anyhow. It seems then I was starting to notice that I may have a problem with my abuse of the drugs and alcohol. My life seemed almost worthless and my only comfort or way I felt any way near normal was when I had some drinks or a line of cocaine here and there.

My old friend Buddy was there on the Caldwell job and we hung out together. One evening after work we went to the local bar to catch happy hour. I loved that happy hour there because they served doubles and two for the price of one. I was into the Black Russians at that time where the double was two shots of Kahlua and four shots of Vodka on ice. With that being a two for one happy hour price this came to 12 shots of straight booze for the first round of drinks. To get my moneys worth and take advantage of the happy hour every day this ritual came to two of those 12 shot happy hour drinks every ten minutes. In an hour this meant pounding down enough booze to equal 72 shots of that wonderful stuff. Happy hour was just that—only an hour long. It came to where I did not remember going home or how I got there or what I did at the bar or after I had left. This was new to me and scary.

Later in the night on one evening shortly after happy hour Buddy and I went for a ride in his old beat up International Scout with no doors, top, or windshield. We were going through the streets of town and I simply fell out of the Scout and into the middle of the street. Buddy didn't realize I was gone for a while but he circled around the block looking for me. I remember laying there in the middle of the street trying to figure out where I was at. I could barely move my body—not because I was hurt but because I was so stoned. There I was lying on my back and I saw the headlights of a car coming toward me. Oh how hard it was to move out of the way—I could not move my body. As the car came closer I remember trying to move and just in time I rolled over there in the street that memorable evening. As I did I could feel the rubber from the tire as it brushed against my head. I thought maybe it was my friend and he would stop but it wasn't. Then another came—I thought it would go around me but no it just seemed to aim right at me. Again I could not move and again just in time I rolled over barely being hit. I wondered if those guys in the cars were drunk or just trying to run over me. Maybe it was both.

Soon Buddy came and helped me back into the Scout. It was not long and he got stopped by the police where they had him taking a field sobriety test. We were parked on a railroad overpass bridge—I looked over the edge and it was a long way down to that railroad track amongst the trees and brush next to it. I then sat on the railing of the bridge and watched as Buddy was taking his sobriety test touching his nose and walking toe to heel. As I sat there on the bridge railing I was trying to be unnoticeable and it was hard for me to keep my balance then I fell backwards off that bridge. I fell through the air and into some trees then down through the branches then some brush and then rolled down a steep hill to the railroad track—this was like a 40 foot drop. It should have killed me but guess I was like a rag doll falling through the air. If I had been sober it probably would have killed me. It was a long trip back up that hill to the bridge and back to the railing. I will never know why Buddy was not thrown in jail but he was still there and didn't even know I was gone. I was all cut up and he got a good laugh—actually we both laughed and went on for some more drinks. It must have been blackout time because I remembered nothing after that. The next morning when I woke up I started to think I may just have been drunk—possibly even have a problem—my life didn't seem to be going to well. I had never really had blackouts like that before where I wake up and do not have a clue of where I was or what I had done. I wondered if I had driven and maybe hit or killed someone with my van. I even looked at the front end to see if there was damage so am thankful I never hurt anyone. Buddy and I went out the next day to a different bar to get a drink but they would not serve me because I had been kicked out the night before and banned from the bar forever. I did not even know why I was kicked out nor even remember being there and still don't. It was such a strange feeling and scary. This may have been the first time in 25 years that I started to really recognize something may be wrong but still not admitting I had a problem. Maybe those little scrapes with death and the blackouts caught my attention just a little because I did think about it.

CHAPTER THIRTEEN

VA Alcohol Drug Treatment Program

I had been hiding out for a year because the court ordered me to go to meetings and classes because of the drunken driving tickets in the previous year. Not to mention the biker guys after me for the business deal gone wrong and my coke dealer wanting paid. Everything with the court was to be completed within a year or else I would go to jail and the year was nearly up—only one week left. One of the stipulations was to go to AA meetings. I went to an AA meeting because I thought I could fool the judge into thinking I had been going for a whole year being just stupid in thinking I could get it all done in a week. The system was not that easy to maneuver and the judge would not be fooled. I was an idiot to even think so.

Reluctantly I went to the AA meeting and listened to a man who told about a situation similar to mine where he had pleaded with the court to go to a program in the VA hospital instead of doing the years classes and meetings or go to jail. This made sense to me and what the heck it was only for a period of 30 days. I thought it is either go to jail or move out of the country or go to the judge and try to do the VA hospital thing. I had already tried to move out of the country with my short time job in Maine and off to Canada for a while. Why not take advantage of the system so it seemed like an easy way out. I had no intention of quitting the alcohol or drugs at all but to just go to the program and do my time. Sure I could fool the court. My plan would be to go into the 30 day program (called ADTP standing for Alcohol Drug Treatment Program) with the VA which would cost me nothing, get out of trouble with the law and then party time when I got out.

Besides the cocaine were doing some strange things to me. When I had been using it at first I would talk and talk, feel really good like on top of the world, felt smart and sexy. It had all changed because when I used coke I would try to speak and no words would come out of my mouth. I would just stand there like an idiot with my mouth open and sort of mumble. I doubt I was very sexy like that. I would feel the paranoia and go off alone and hide under anything to get away from people. I still wanted the coke though and drank more booze than ever.

Buddy had quit smoking. Cigarettes and any other thing I would smoke made me cough and gag. Guess it was because of the three or four packs a day then with those Lucky Strike straights, the cocaine and the booze. My lips were sore and bleeding from the paper of the cigarettes ripping the skin off my lips. With that and feeling I could quit if he did I attempted to stop smoking. With the help of a small amount of desire a little competition and a lot of Nicorette I had quit smoking. Actually being pretty pleased with myself after 25 years of sucking on those things. Yup Buddy quit smoking and I was able to do the same but—I saw this little round circle in the back pocket of his jeans—the guy was chewing tobacco. Buddy was cheating on the chewbaccy—the rascal. For some reason I continued to quit the cigarettes.

I contacted the VA in Boise and they said there would be an hour long meeting and then if they felt there was an alcohol or drug related problem they would then submit it to the staff and let me know in a few weeks of their decision if I would be admitted to the Alcohol Drug Treatment Program. Much to my surprise I was generously accepted after a fifteen minute interview and no staff meeting. The program was to start about 60 days after acceptance but I was admitted in a couple of weeks. Maybe they thought I was a real drug addicted alcoholic even though they did not know I had other plans. I made a deal with the judge to go to the VA hospital in lieu of the other classes and treatment and she accepted it. One requirement was to be admitted sober with nothing to drink three days prior to admittance. I managed to make it a few hours before admittance. As all the guys I worked with drank and either dealt or used cocaine I figured I had better quit my job a few days before the hospital or I would never make it so I quit the job.

I was the only one in the alcohol/drug treatment program who did not smoke, even the staff workers were smokers. I went into the Alcohol Drug Treatment program smoke free on the 21st day of November 1985 at the ripe old age of 42 and was told to enter the doors there sober. I thought I was sober but there was a mandatory test to determine if the new or existing "inmates" were sober. I was legally intoxicated and had signs of cocaine and marijuana in my body. They said it would probably show up for the next 3 days and if it continued to show up I would be expelled from the program. I really wanted to go through the program because I did not want to go to jail. Besides it was a warm place to stay instead of the cold van out in the winter snow. There were even showers and free meals and a real bed to sleep in.

After 3 days my tests came out that I was sober. Hmmmmmm the first time in 25 years that I could remember being sober. It was really different. Yes I was starting to notice I was a selfish person, selfish to my ex wife and my children and everyone else and to my self. I started to feel I needed to be honest with myself. People had always called me a nice guy. The girls I knew would not trust me because they thought I was too nice because they felt I was hiding something by being nice. So what could be so wrong being a nice guy or maybe it was just the people I chose for my friends. They gave me a physical and found poisoning (cirrhosis) in my liver from the alcohol. They said it could possibly clear up in a couple of weeks and if it did not then I would probably live for maybe a year and it would be fatal—end of story. I really didn't care.

There were classes every day and they had an exercise program and then more classes but no personal therapist like all of the other guys. I asked the supervisor why. He said they felt I could do better by learning on my own. I was disappointed because I was actually starting to think maybe I had been a drunk, a cocaine addict, one of the low lives of the earth and someone would offer to help me so what's new anyhow.

During the program they talked about a higher power and that our higher power could be anyone or anything we wanted it to be. I remembered the scripture "For God so loved the world that he gave his only begotten son for whosoever believeth in him, shall not perish but have everlasting life" which I remembered from when I went to church as a little guy. I decided to have Jesus be my fictitious "Higher Power" and just let it go at that. Who ever this was and he really pissed me off anyhow because he let me have such a crappy life.

I started feeling better in that hospital than I ever had in my entire life for as long as I could ever remember. Have heard about withdrawals and wondered why this was not happening to me because I did not get sick. It was interesting that I could feel good without the drugs or alcohol. During one of the classes it was stated by the instructor "*Your very worse day sober will be better than your very best day when you were drinking*". I got to thinking about that. Then the instructor told us the definition of an alcoholic. I really never knew. He said it was *someone who drank and experienced problems in their life from the use of alcohol.* I got to thinking about that too. It was starting to make some sense. He said some became alcoholic after the first drink. I wondered if I was one of those special few. At that point I was thinking that I might even stop drinking and just use some really high quality marijuana and keep up with the cocaine as usual.

CHAPTER FOURTEEN

Thanksgiving

28 November 1985 was Thanksgiving Day and I had been in the program for 7 days then. It was cold and was snowing fiercely. There was about a foot of that fluffy white stuff on the ground around the Veterans Hospital. Normally I did not like the snow but this day I loved the purity, the whiteness, how it was all fluffy and clean looking—when the sun came out it glittered like a freshly cut diamond in a perfect setting. Everyone in the program to include the staff and the patients was to take the Thanksgiving holiday off and spend time with their families. The staff and all of the patients were gone. I really had nobody to go to and I did not have time to go and visit my mother in Oregon and besides I had no money because I gave it to my old friend Buddy. It was a couple of hundred

dollars I had saved for when I got out of the hospital. He was kind enough to keep it for me safe from the derelicts that would be in the hospital with me.

The staff said I could stay at the hospital with a few others who had no place to go. I really thought about skipping out and get some drinks somewhere or find one of my buddies and go party but decided to stick it out for four days because I knew for a fact if I left then I would never come back. Just didn't want to go to jail and it was really different being sober for a couple of days and I was starting to like it. The psychiatric wing being next to the treatment program area was staffed with a nurse's station and there was a cafeteria for meals so there I was pretty much alone in the ADTP wing of the VA hospital for Thanksgiving weekend for four days. I was asked not to leave because there was nobody there to monitor or test me for alcohol or drugs for when I would get back. I did not want to risk the possibility of getting kicked out of the program as I already had a good start on it.

I started enjoying my time alone and was even enjoying my time being sober. I had thought one could not have fun or enjoy themselves or even function without the alcohol or drugs. Surprise—I was reading a few books and I hated to read. I was writing some poetry just for kicks which actually made sense. There was a nice Thanksgiving dinner at the hospital at least for an Army hospital. Any kind of a complete meal for me would have been unusual because I had not eaten an actual meal for years. I was 5' 11" and weighed about 140 pounds and a big belly so it probably showed. My unshaved face was red from the liver poisoning and my clothes were like rags and my hair was a mess so I was not a pretty sight. Any money was spent on booze and drugs so my priorities were not for other comforts or needs.

CHAPTER FIFTEEN

Admitted Problem Then a Miracle

The evening approached darkness that Thanksgiving Day Thursday evening and the skies were clear but you could see that darkness rolling in which would normally be followed by a storm. There was no wind outside—it was calm. It was around 8:00 in the evening and I felt good from the Thanksgiving dinner from down at the hospital cafeteria. I went to my room which was a large room about 15' x 30' housing 8 Army beds all covered with those dark brown wool blankets used by the GI's for centuries. There was a foot locker set at the end of each of the beds for personal belongings. The Veterans Hospital was built in 1863 during the civil war so it was not a modern hospital as one would expect. The room had one door to enter from the end of a large long hallway which went the length of the wing and then around the corner was the psychiatric ward. The end wall being 30' in length consisted of huge windows with square glass panes. The windows were about 3' off the floor and went high up to the tall ceiling of that old room. Outside the windows were a courtyard for about 30' and then past that were an outdoor storage area and some parking for equipment.

I went over to the windows and looked down at the courtyard. From the third floor it seemed a long way down to the fluffy white snow. By then it was snowing like crazy and I stood there and looked at the huge snowflakes gently dancing to the ground. There was a light on a pole out by the parking lot which I looked down upon. It gave only minimal light and lit up the ground just enough to see through the darkness which was adorned with the glittering snowflakes. For some reason I could not keep away from the window and look at the snow. It was beautiful out there. I don't know how long I stood there. There was one of those old school house lights hanging in the center of the room but I had not turned it on. It was dark in the room but there was enough light coming through the windows where I could see enough to get around.

It was around 9:00 in the evening by then. There was nobody around but I did not feel lonely. It was cold but

I was warm inside. There I was in that huge hospital experiencing something I had never experienced in my life. My troubles were left somewhere outside of that room and for some reason I was comforted but at the same time I felt anger inside of me. I briefly looked back at my past and thought, why did I have to go through such a miserable life?

At that moment I admitted the booze and drugs were causing problems in my life. I thought about the "higher power" which was talked about in the program. My hospital Army cot was in the back corner of the large room away from the windows. I sat on the cot with my feet on the bed and leaned against the wall behind the bed. Again I remembered about the "higher power" and how I chose Jesus for my higher power. Again I felt angry about how my life was a mess and how I had lived in such a garbage dump for it seemed my whole life. I didn't know how to pray but I thought why not?

I spoke out loud—there was nobody there to listen—but I was a little pissed off I guess because I was feeling sorry for myself and said with anger "Jesus Christ" I am tired of all this! I have a problem; please help me get off of the booze and the drugs! Help me to have a decent life! Before the last word was out of my mouth the room started to slowly fill up with this very bright and direct light. I looked toward the windows and the light came through the windows. The light was white and even more pure than the snow I was focusing on just before. It came through the middle of the windows and it was a small light about two feet around and as the light entered through the window it stopped right there in the middle of that room. Within a few seconds that light began to fill up the entire room with the brightest in the center of the room. That room was so filled up with this light that there was no darkness at all. The light was brighter than any light I have ever seen, it was even brighter than the light of an electric welding arc but it did not hurt my eyes and was not harsh but comforting. It was soft like a cloud and I can never really explain of the whiteness and the brightness of that light. I guess the light just felt clean. I was filled with fear of that unknown and scared as hell but still was filled with a great peace all at the same time. As the light filled the room there was a voice which came from the center of that room and the voice was magnificently clear and precise. There was no person there for the voice to come from but there was still this bright light in the center of the room. The voice called me by name and said these words I will never forget **"GARY—YOU ARE READY"**. It was just that simple. Within only a few seconds the light slowly withdrew from the room and I could see the darkness again.

I was astonished, happy and scared all at the same time. I got up from the Army cot and went out the door and down the hall running like a mad man. I went around the corner and there was the nurse's station to the right for the psychiatric ward. I ran up to the two nurses on duty and said "Did you see that?" Did you hear that?" It was quiet and gloomy in that hall there and the nurses looked at me like I was some kind of a crazy nut. They said they didn't see or hear anything—they asked if I would like to go and talk to someone about it. Oh crap they were ready to throw me into the crazy ward of the hospital. I said no never mind, have a nice Thanksgiving and I turned away and walked back (apprehensively) to the room pretending to be calm. Only just a little confused trying to fool the nurses that I was not a whacko and what I had just experienced.

Twenty five years have passed since that incident and I have not taken any booze or drugs since that moment. I have not once craved for the booze or drugs to this day however coming pretty close a few times. I have always felt that Jesus himself with his ever so busy schedule took time from his day to save me. I feel of him not as just a spirit but my close friend.

All I had to do was to **ADMIT** I had a problem and then there was a way to make the addiction go away. I was happier than I had ever been in my entire life. This was my "Higher Power" and yours could be the same or anything you want it to be. It could be a star, a person, Buddha, a cloud, the heavens, the sky or a mountain or what ever you want as your higher power. That would be your decision but having this "higher power" sure clinched the deal for me.

CHAPTER SIXTEEN

Back to Life

I left the hospital with my van as my home, sober, with a clean liver, a clean body, a smile on my face and about $20 in my pocket. I had no intentions of drinking or doing any drugs. I had no job but knew it would work out. I stopped by a few of my old Boise friends and told them of how I was sorry for my actions when I had been drinking and also excited to tell them I had given up on the drugs and booze. They really had no clue what I was talking about and they said lets go down to the Outlaw Club.

I then thought of what the counselor said in the treatment center. *"Your very worse day sober will be better than your very best day when you were drinking"*. I felt really felt good. I also remembered hearing in the treatment center that I needed to *"Change playmates and playgrounds"*. At that time it seemed to make sense to me so I just said I have to go now. Never saw those people again. The old friends told me that the biker guys who were looking for me heard that I was dead so that eased my mind. My drug dealer was part of that crowd as well so he probably thought the same.

The next place I went was to visit Buddy who was driving the Scout the night I fell onto the train tracks, the same friend who enticed me to stop smoking, and the same friend who I entrusted my couple of hundred bucks to, the same friend who I first got drunk with when I was a junior in High School. He was the same one who was there when I started to be aware of my addiction even though he did not know it. I went to get my money from him in Ontario Oregon which was only about 50 miles from the hospital. I still remember the look on his face as I asked for my money. He acted like he had been caught with his hand in the cookie jar or should I say the cocaine jar. He made excuses and asked me to come back later. Being persistent he finally told me he had spent all of my money on drugs and that he could give me $20.00. He said I was an idiot to trust someone like him with my life savings. Guess I was.

I took the $20 and went on down the road to stay with my mother in Prineville. She was so pleased that

I had stopped drinking. She said she had tried to talk to me about it many times but she felt I had to do it on my own. I told her I wish she had said something a long time ago. Of course it probably would not have made any difference because it was my problem and I needed to recognize it and admit there was a problem before it could be solved—nobody else could. My life was changed, I was happy and the guy was right about my worse day sober would be better than my best day drunk. I was now able to say that I had been a drunk. I could not get the smile off of my face.

I picked up some little odd jobs to gain some money. I fixed up my van on the interior to make it a nicer place to live—yes life was awesome. I worked as a surveyor and as a laborer in Lakeview Oregon and saved up a little cash. Literally all the other guys on the job would go to the bar every night after work and drink. They never asked me to go along—I was so proud that I had quit drinking that I told everyone about it. They called me a weirdo and laughed at me but I did not care.

I went to a few churches there in Lakeview but nothing seemed to be right for me—even one preacher giving this sermon said that anyone who ever had done drugs would go to hell and if one ever dealt drugs they would have a sure one way ticket to Hell. I did not believe a word of it because I knew Jesus loved me which was why I was there that day—alive and sober. What an exciting time of my life—I felt like I was 15 years old again and here I was 42. My next stop was to Eugene Oregon where I got a job for only a week. The company decided to not pursue its desire for developing a healthy dog food labeled Growl-nola.

I was heading back to Prineville from Eugene in my orange van trailed by a cloud of smoke from the exhaust . . . . It was in the fall and the leaves on the trees were changing color. I would look through the trees and I could see all the beauty there. I could see shining streams of light pouring between the open spots between the leaves. I had never noticed these kinds of things before. I was so full of happiness that I cried out loud "Thank You"! Thanks for saving my life! Thanks for helping me get sober! Thanks for being with me! Thank you for all of this beauty! At those moments I felt just as close to Jesus my higher power as I did the day he visited me in the hospital. Those leaves of green, yellow, red and orange seemed to burst out in the suns rays as I cruised past Belknap Hot springs and nearly to Shelilah Falls. I just couldn't stand to continue without stopping and soaking in the feelings which I was experiencing. All that beauty which surrounded me felt so new to me and clean and pure. I felt like a child experiencing many new things.

There I was in the parking lot of Shelilah Falls and walked down to the falls. The sun was glistening everywhere through the trees and the leaves. It was like lightening blasting through each of the little drops of water exploding through the air around the falls. I went back to my orange van and got my camera so I could "capture the moment". Of course my antique 127 Kodak was nearly impossible to aim at the subject as I looked down into the bent up prism lens.

Nearly a year later I had developed the film and was shocked to only see some old cans and beer bottles lying on the ground. The camera took a photo of the ground because of the lens not being in line with the camera. I smiled and then laughed as I looked at the picture. Of course only I would understand what I saw in the picture that day. Yes there was a picture of garbage on the ground but I saw past the garbage and saw the real beauty on this earth for us to enjoy. It was even fun to just look at the stars up in the heavens and daydream of what was up there and how all of this came about. It was time to start life over again. My home building business came back to me easily and within a few years was back building homes and experiencing a new life.

I became aware and admitted there was a problem, then went for help and got sober, that simple. My life started all over again. 25 years later and still sober. This was *my trip to "Halfway to Hell and Back".* I don't want to take that trip ever again. Been close a few times but never made that fatal turn yet. Still one second at a time and loving it!

Are you ready to come back?